My
AMAZING
Body

RACHEL WRIGHT

TWO CAN ™

LONDON ■ PRINCETON

How to use this book

Cross references
Above the heading on the page, you will find a list of subjects in the book which are connected to the topic. Look at these pages to find out more about the subjects.

See for yourself
See for yourself bubbles give you the chance to test out some of the ideas in this book. They explain what you will need and what you have to do to see if an idea really works.

Quiz corner
In the quiz corner, you will find a list of questions. The answers to the quiz questions are somewhere on the two pages. Can you answer all the questions about each topic?

Glossary
Difficult words are explained in the glossary near the back of the book. These words are in **bold** on the page. Look them up in the glossary to find out what they mean.

Index
The index is at the back of the book. It is a list of words about everything mentioned in the book, with page numbers next to the words. The list is in the same order as the alphabet. If you want to find out about a subject, look up the word in the index, then turn to the page number given.

Contents

Your amazing body

Your body is an amazing machine. It can move, think, listen and talk. It also mends itself, changes shape and grows. Your body is made of lots of different parts, all working together. You can see some parts, such as your skin and hair. Others, such as your **brain** and **bones**, are hidden inside you.

Before you were born
You started your life inside your mother's tummy. At first you were just a tiny speck, about the size of a full stop. Then you grew and grew, until you were ready to be born.

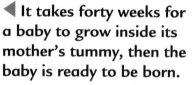 It takes forty weeks for a baby to grow inside its mother's tummy, then the baby is ready to be born.

Growing up
When you were growing from a baby into a toddler, your body changed quickly. You grew about 20cm a year. You are still growing and changing now, but much more slowly. At seven years old, you grow about 6cm taller each year. When you are a teenager, your body will start to grow and change faster again.

Growing older

Many people stay healthy all through their grown-up years. They take care of their bodies by keeping fit, eating well and taking time to relax.

▼ Older adults often spend time doing the things they enjoy most, such as playing with grandchildren.

▲ As you grow older, your body becomes stronger and you can run faster.

Teenagers

Between the ages of about ten and fourteen, your body will grow taller and change shape. By the time you are about twenty, you will be fully grown.

As girls grow up, they become more rounded, like their mothers. Boys develop broader shoulders and their voices become deeper. Both girls and boys become more hairy as they grow older.

Quiz Corner

- What happens to your body between the ages of ten and fourteen?

- At about what age are you fully grown?

- What happens to a boy's voice as he grows older?

- How can you stay healthy all your life?

look at: Your muscles, page 8, Breathing, page 12

Your skeleton

Inside your body, there is a strong framework of 206 **bones** called a skeleton. Your skeleton gives your body its shape and strength. If you didn't have a skeleton, you would be as floppy as a bean bag. Your skeleton also helps to protect fragile parts inside your body.

Inside bones

Your bones are not dead and dried up. They are alive, just like the rest of you. Your bones are hard and solid on the outside, but inside many of them have a fatty jelly called bone marrow. Bone marrow helps to make your **blood**.

bone

marrow

CHATTERBOX

Insects and crabs don't have a skeleton inside their bodies. Instead they have a hard outer shell, called an exoskeleton, which protects their soft insides.

▼ Some of the bones in your skeleton are tiny. Others are long and strong.

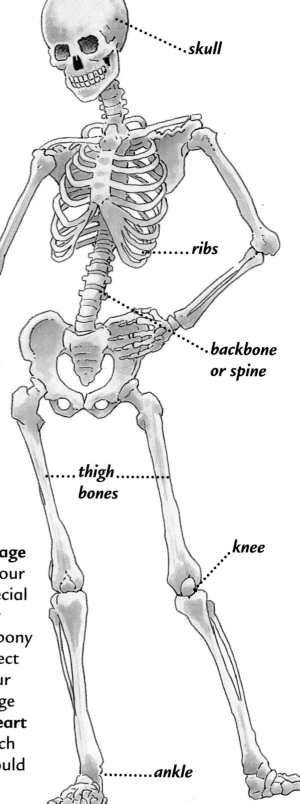

skull

ribs

backbone or spine

thigh bones

knee

ankle

Skull and rib cage
Each bone in your body has a special job to do. Your skull makes a bony helmet to protect your **brain**. Your ribs make a cage around your **heart** and **lungs**, which are soft and could be hurt easily.

Joints

Wherever bones meet in the skeleton, you have a joint. Your knees are hinge joints. They let you move your legs up and down. Your shoulders are ball and socket joints. They let you move your arms in circles.

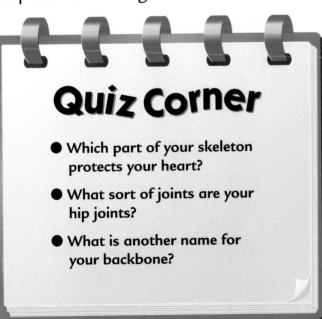

▲ Your spine is bendy because it is made up of lots of little bones and joints.

Broken bones

If you break a bone, new bone grows to join the broken ends together. A hard bandage called a plaster cast helps to keep the bone straight while it mends.

Quiz Corner

● Which part of your skeleton protects your heart?

● What sort of joints are your hip joints?

● What is another name for your backbone?

▼ You can bend, twist and turn your body because you have joints between your bones.

Finger joints are called knuckles.

Shoulders are ball and socket joints.

Elbows are hinge joints.

Hips are ball and socket joints.

Knees are hinge joints.

Toes have hinge joints.

look at: Your skeleton, page 6, Your brain, page 16

Your muscles

Muscles make your body move. Many of your muscles are fixed to the **bones** of your skeleton by strong straps, called tendons. Every time you run, jump or walk, lots of these muscles pull on your bones. This makes your bones move, which makes your body move.

▼ Your muscles will stay fit and strong if you make them work hard by playing energetic games.

Pairs of muscles

Many of your muscles work in pairs. One muscle pulls a bone one way, then its partner pulls the bone back again.

When you bend your elbow, your biceps muscle becomes shorter, pulling your arm up.

biceps

triceps

When you straighten your arm, your triceps muscle becomes shorter, pulling your arm down.

Sending messages

Your **brain** controls your muscles. It works out which muscles you need to move each part of your body. Your brain sends messages to your muscles to pull on your bones. Then, when your muscles have pulled, they send messages back to your brain.

Pulling faces

Not all your muscles pull on bones. Some of the muscles in your face pull on your skin. You use these muscles every time you smile, frown, or pull a funny face.

▲ Every time you frown, your body uses more than 40 muscles. A smile uses only about 15 muscles. So if you want to save muscle power – smile!

Different muscles

You have three different types of muscle in your body. Each type has a different job to do. One type pulls your bones, to make you move. Another type pushes your food through your body and a third type makes your **heart** beat.

Quiz Corner

- What do muscles help you to do?

- Why are energetic games good for you?

- How many different types of muscles are there in your body?

- Which uses more muscles – a smile or a frown?

look at: Blood, page 14, Taking care of yourself, page 28

Eating

Your body needs food to help it grow and work properly. But your body cannot use the food you eat just as it is. Food has to be chewed and chopped up, then changed inside you, until it is small enough to pass into your **blood**. Then your blood can carry it to all the different parts of your body.

Food tubes
Inside your body, there is a long tube which goes from your mouth all the way to your bottom. The top part of this tube is fairly straight, but the bottom part is wiggly. Different things happen to your food as it travels through each part of this tube.

◀ Your body takes all the goodness it needs from your food, then it pushes out the **waste**.

CHATTERBOX

Snakes don't chew their food the way you do. When an egg-eating snake spies a tasty looking egg, it opens its mouth wide and swallows the egg whole.

10

Healthy eating

You need to eat small amounts of lots of different kinds of foods to give you **energy** and to help you grow. Eggs, meat and fish all help you grow. Bread and pasta give you energy. Fruit and vegetables are full of **vitamins and minerals.**

.....When you chew, your teeth chop up your food and your spit makes it soft enough for you to swallow.

.... After you swallow, your food is pushed along this part of your food tube into your stomach.

.... Inside your stomach, your food is broken down by strong juices and turned into a thick, soupy mush.

*..... By now, the useful bits of your food are very tiny. They pass through the sides of the tube and into nearby **blood vessels.***

..... Any leftover bits of food that your body cannot use are squeezed along to the end of your food tube. You push them out of your body when you go to the toilet.

▼ Babies don't have any teeth to chew their food, so baby food is usually soft and easy to swallow.

◀ Your body is made up mostly of water. Every day, you need to drink fresh water to stay healthy. Your body tells you when to drink by making you feel thirsty.

Quiz Corner

- Why do you need to eat?
- What happens to food in your stomach?
- Which foods give you energy?
- When do you feel thirsty?
- Why is baby food soft?

look at: Blood, page 14

Breathing

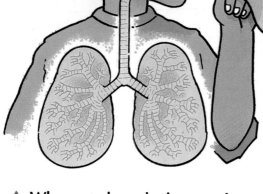

You need to breathe to stay alive. When you breathe in, you suck air into your body through your nose and mouth. The air goes down a tube in your neck, then into your **lungs**. Your lungs are stretchy bags that fill up with air, in the same way as a sponge fills with water.

▲ When you breathe in, your lungs become bigger as they fill up with air.

Oxygen

In the air around you, there is an invisible gas called **oxygen**. Every time you breathe in, you take oxygen into your lungs. Inside your lungs, oxygen seeps into tubes filled with **blood**. Then your blood carries the oxygen all around your body.

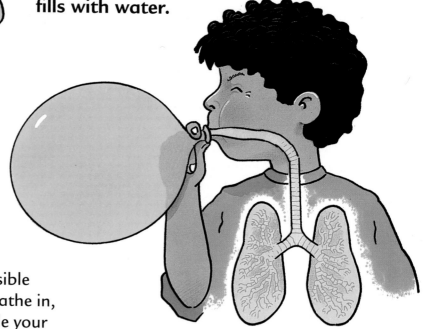

▲ When you breathe out, your lungs become smaller as you push out the air. This air can blow up a balloon.

SEE FOR YOURSELF

When you breathe in, your chest becomes bigger to make room for your lungs. When you breathe out, your chest becomes smaller again. Cross your arms like this and take a deep breath in and out. Can you feel your chest moving?

Breathing out

As your body uses up oxygen, it makes a gas, called **carbon dioxide**. This gas is a **waste** product, which means it is not needed in your body. Your blood carries this gas back to your lungs, so that you can breathe it out. All day and night, you breathe in oxygen and breathe out carbon dioxide.

▼ Fish can breathe underwater, but people cannot. Scuba divers have to carry tanks filled with oxygen on their backs.

Quiz Corner

- What is oxygen?
- How does oxygen get into your body?
- What happens to your chest as you breathe in and out?
- How do divers breathe underwater?

look at: Your muscles, page 8, Eating, page 10, Breathing, page 12

Blood

▼ Your heart pumps blood around your body.

Blood is a thick liquid which flows round and round your body. It carries goodness from the food you eat and **oxygen** from the air you breathe to every part of your body. It also picks up **waste** that your body doesn't need and takes it to parts of your body that can get rid of it.

Blood vessels

Blood travels around your body in rubbery pipes called **blood vessels**. These blood vessels run from your **heart** to your **lungs**, then all the way around your body and back again. Sometimes you can see your blood vessels through your skin. They look similar to thin blue lines.

Your busy heart

Your heart is a special **muscle** inside your chest. Its job is to keep blood moving around your body. Each time your heart squeezes, it pushes blood through your blood vessels. It does this all day and all night without stopping for a rest.

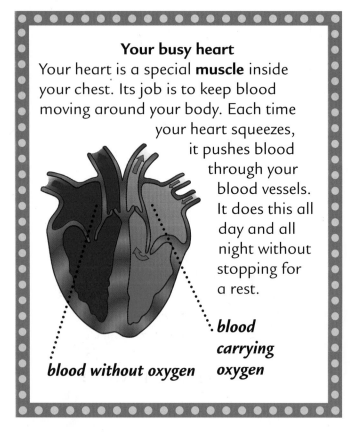

blood without oxygen

blood carrying oxygen

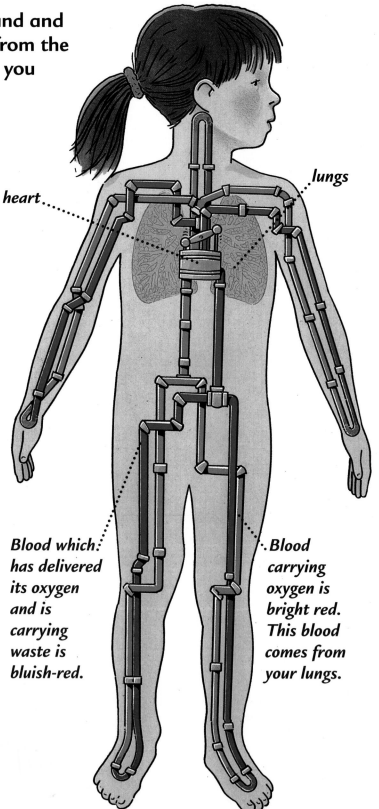

heart

lungs

Blood which has delivered its oxygen and is carrying waste is bluish-red.

Blood carrying oxygen is bright red. This blood comes from your lungs.

New skin

If you cut yourself, thick blood plugs up the hole. Over time, the plug hardens to make a scab. New skin grows under the scab, then the scab falls off.

If you stretched out all the blood vessels in your body and laid them end to end, they would be almost long enough to go round the Earth three times.

▲ A sticking plaster helps to stop germs getting into your body through a cut. It keeps the cut clean until the skin mends.

Quiz Corner

● Name three things that blood does.

● What colour is blood with oxygen in it?

● What does your heart do all day and night?

● What happens when you cut yourself?

Fighting germs

Your blood also helps your body to fight **germs**. Germs are tiny living things that can make you sick when they live inside your body. Special **cells** in your blood, called **white blood cells**, fight these harmful germs and help to make you feel well again.

15

look at: Your muscles, page 8, Breathing, page 12, Hearing, page 18, Seeing, page 20, Touching, page 24

Your brain

Inside your head, there is a soft pinky-grey lump protected by your skull. This is your **brain**. Your brain controls your whole body. It tells your **muscles** and **senses** what to do. It also does all your thinking, learning and remembering.

Network of nerves
Your brain is linked to every part of your body by pathways called **nerves**. Your brain sends messages all over your body along these pathways. Different parts of your body also use this network to send messages back to your brain.

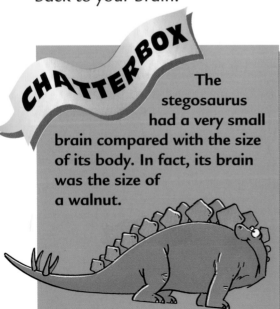

CHATTERBOX The stegosaurus had a very small brain compared with the size of its body. In fact, its brain was the size of a walnut.

▲ This is what the outer layer of your brain looks like. Different parts of your outer brain have different jobs to do.

*This part of your brain sends nerve messages to your muscles. It tells them to pull on your **bones** so that you can move.*

This part of your brain controls your speech. It helps you talk to your friends.

This part of your brain receives nerve messages from your eyes. Then it lets you know what you are looking at.

This part of your brain sorts out the nerve messages from your ears. It tells you what you are listening to.

Your brain stem controls things you do which you don't have to think about, such as breathing and sneezing.

Dreams

Your brain works all day and all night. Even when you are asleep, it controls your heartbeat and breathing. Your brain also carries on thinking while you are sleeping. Sometimes you remember these night thoughts as dreams.

▲ Dreams usually last for about half an hour. Most people have about four dreams each night, but don't always remember them.

Quiz Corner

● How long do dreams usually last?

● What does your brain do?

● Your brain is linked to the rest of your body by pathways. What are these pathways called?

look at: Your brain, page 16

Hearing

Hearing is one of your five main **senses**. The others are seeing, smelling, tasting and touching. Your sense of hearing lets you hear many different sounds, from a pin dropping to an elephant trumpeting. It lets you enjoy your favourite music. It can also warn you of many dangers that you cannot see, such as a car speeding up behind you.

Looking at ears

The two flaps on the sides of your head are only part of your ears. The rest of your ears are safe inside your head, covered up by your hard bony skull.

Inside your ears

Your ear flaps are similar to the wide end of a funnel. They catch sounds from the air which go into your ears. In your inner ear, the sounds are turned into messages. These messages whizz along **nerves** to your **brain**. Your brain then tells you what you are listening to.

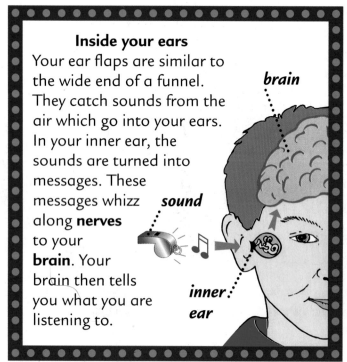

brain

sound

inner ear

▲ Your brain sorts out the sounds you hear. You can tell the difference between the sounds of all kinds of musical instruments.

Many animals can waggle their ear flaps. This means that they can work out where sounds are coming from without turning their heads and attracting enemies.

Silent talk

Often, people who cannot hear learn to talk using special hand signs to spell out and show different words and sentences. This way of talking is called signing.

▲ These children are using signs to talk. The girl is saying that she is tired and the boy wants to know what the time is.

Quiz Corner

● Why is hearing so useful?

● Which part of your body protects your inner ears?

● What can a rabbit do with its ears that you can't?

● How do people who cannot hear talk to each other?

look at: Your brain, page 16

Seeing

Your eyes need light to see. Light bounces off everything you look at and goes into each eye through the small black hole in the middle. Messages about the light are sent along a **nerve** to your **brain** which makes sense of what you see.

▼ Sight is one of your five main **senses**. It gives you a picture of what is happening in the world around you.

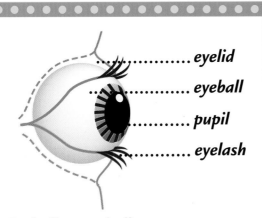

eyelid
eyeball
pupil
eyelash

Eyeball to eyeball

Each of your eyes is similar to a squashy ping pong ball. When you look in the mirror you see only the front of your eyes. The rest of each eye is inside your head.

Letting in light

The black hole in the middle of each eye is called the pupil. In dim light, your pupils become bigger to let more light into your eyes. In bright light, your pupils shrink to protect your eyes.

SEE FOR YOURSELF

Ask a friend to stand in a dark room. Look at one of his pupils. Now turn on the light. What do you notice?

Keeping your eyes clean

Salty tears help to keep your eyes clean and wet. You also make tears when you feel unhappy, but nobody knows why.

Wearing glasses

Some people can see things clearly only if they are close by. These people are short-sighted. Others can see things clearly only if they are far away. They are long-sighted. Wearing glasses can help to correct these problems.

Quiz Corner

- What are the black holes in the middle of your eyes called?

- Why do these holes become bigger in dim light?

- What do tears help to do?

- What things can you see clearly if you are short-sighted?

look at: Eating, page 10, Your brain, page 16

Smelling and tasting

Smell and taste are two of your **senses**. When you eat, your tongue picks up tastes and your nose picks up smells. This lets you enjoy the full flavour of your food. Sometimes smells cannot get into your nose because it is blocked by a cold. When this happens, you cannot taste properly.

Inside your nose

Inside your head, the holes leading from your mouth and nose join up. When you eat, smells from your food go up the back of your mouth and into your nose. Inside your nose, smell collectors pick up these smells and send messages about them to your **brain**.

Smells in the air

Your nose doesn't just help your tongue with tasting. It also picks up smells floating in the air around you. Smells are invisible, like the air. When you breathe in, they go up your nose.

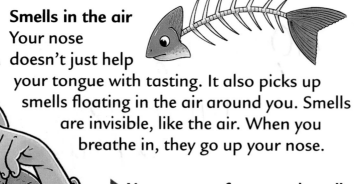

▶ Your senses of taste and smell tell you if food is good or bad to eat. Fresh food tastes and smells delicious. Rotten food tastes and smells horrid.

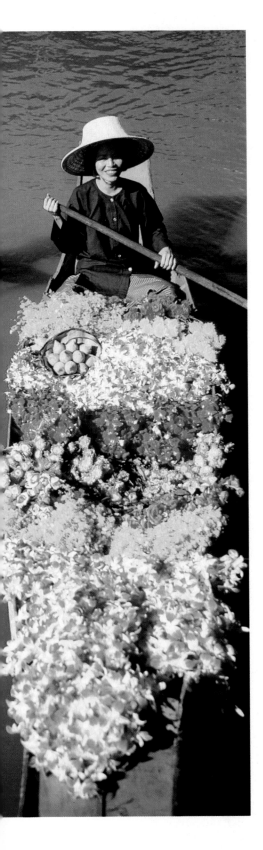

Taste buds

Your tongue is covered in tiny bumps, called taste buds. Taste buds at the front of your tongue pick up sweet and salty flavours. Those on the sides sense sour tastes, such as lemon. Those at the back pick up bitter tastes, such as coffee grains.

This part picks up sour tastes.

This part picks up sweet and salty tastes.

This part picks up bitter tastes.

SEE FOR YOURSELF

Try this test to see how much stronger your sense of smell is than your sense of taste. First blindfold a friend. Now hold an onion under her nose and feed her some bread. What does your friend think she is eating?

Quiz Corner

- Why can't you taste your food properly when your nose is blocked?

- Which four tastes can your taste buds pick up?

- Why are your senses of taste and smell useful?

look at: Your brain, page 16, Skin, page 26

Touching

Your **sense** of touch lets you know how things feel against your skin. When you stroke something with your hand, **nerves** in your skin send messages about the feeling to your **brain**. If the feeling is horrible or unfamiliar, your brain tells you to snatch your hand away. If the feeling is safe and soft, your brain lets you leave your hand where it is.

▶ Stroking the soft fur of a pet is a great feeling. So is giving a cuddle to someone you love.

SEE FOR YOURSELF

Here's a way to test a friend's sense of touch. Make a hole in the side of a box and ask a friend to stick his hand through it. Now put different things, such as cold spaghetti, a potato and a leaf, inside the box. Can your friend guess what each thing is just by touching it?

24

Different feelings

Your sense of touch tells you if something is hot or cold, hard or soft, rough or smooth. It also lets you know if something is hurting you. Pain is useful because it lets you know when something is harming your body.

▲ Your sense of touch warns you if a drink is hot or cold. It also tells you if things are wet.

▲ When you stand on a drawing pin, a sharp pain tells you to take your foot away.

▲ When you shake hands, you can feel your friend's hand pressing against yours.

◄ A pineapple's skin feels rough and hard, but an apple's skin feels smooth.

Tongue, lips and fingertips

Some parts of your skin feel things more clearly than others because they have more nerve endings. Your fingertips, tongue and lips have lots of nerve endings. This is why a baby often feels things with its mouth.

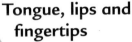

▲ Often, a baby finds out what shape a toy is by putting it in its mouth.

Quiz Corner

- Which part of your body feels things more clearly – the back of your hand or the tips of your fingers?

- Why is pain useful?

- Why does a baby often put things in its mouth?

25

look at: Touching, page 24

Skin

Your skin is like a stretchy, washable, showerproof suit that covers you from head to toe. It helps stop harmful things from getting into your body. It also works hard to keep you at the right **temperature**.

▶ Your skin stops water soaking into your body. It also stops the inside of your body from drying out in the sun.

Skin colour

Everyone's skin has a kind of dye, or colour, called melanin. Melanin helps to protect skin from the sun's harmful rays. People with dark skin have more melanin than people with fair skin. This means that dark skin is better protected from the sun than fair skin. In sunny weather, skin makes more melanin to protect itself. This is why your skin may become darker in the sun.

Sweat

Your skin is covered in tiny holes called pores. When you are very hot, salty water, called sweat, comes out of the pores. As the sweat dries, it takes heat away from your skin. This helps to cool you down.

CHATTERBOX

Reptiles, such as geckos and snakes, cannot sweat to keep cool. Instead, when they are hot, they have to lie in a shady spot and wait until they cool down.

Save your skin

Too much sunshine can burn and damage your skin. If you want to have fun in the sun safely, follow these rules.

● Wear a wide-brimmed hat to protect your face.

● Use sun cream on any parts of your body not covered up by clothes.

Looking at hair

Hair grows all over your skin, except on your lips, the soles of your feet and the palms of your hands. In some places your hairs are easy to see. In others, they are so tiny, you have to look closely to find them.

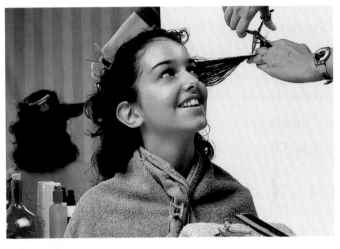

▲ The hair on your head grows faster than the hair on the rest of your body.

Having a haircut

The roots of your hair, which are inside your skin, are alive and growing. But the part of your hair that you can see is dead. This is why having a haircut doesn't hurt.

Quiz Corner

● Why do you sweat when you are hot?

● How can you save your skin from sunburn?

● Which part of your hair is alive?

● Where doesn't your hair grow?

look at: Your muscles, page 8, Eating, page 10

Taking care of yourself

There are lots of ways of taking care of yourself. Eating the right food is one way. Getting enough sleep and exercise are other ways. Washing your body, cleaning your teeth and combing your hair each day are important too. This is because keeping clean makes you look, feel and smell good.

Sugar alert

Sugary foods and drinks are great for a treat and give you an instant boost of **energy**. But to keep healthy, you should eat a mixture of all the different types of foods, including plenty of fresh fruit and vegetables.

Grown-up teeth

At about the age of six, you start to lose your first set of teeth. One by one, your second set of teeth grow in their place. You have only one set of grown-up teeth, so make sure you take care of them.

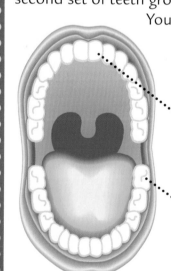

Your front teeth are for biting and tearing food.

Your back teeth are for grinding and chewing food.

Keeping happy and healthy
Playing football, going for a walk, running and swimming are all kinds of exercise. Taking exercise regularly helps to keep your body fit and strong. It's good fun too.

Now wash your hands
You should always wash your hands before eating or touching food. This stops any **germs** that might be on your hands from getting on to your food and making you ill.

▲ Playing outside with friends is a good way to exercise.

◀ To wash yourself really well you need to use soap and clean water. The soap loosens the greasy dirt on your skin and the water washes it away.

Quiz Corner

● What can you do to take care of yourself?

● How many sets of teeth do you have in your lifetime?

● Why should you wash your hands before meals?

● How does soap work?

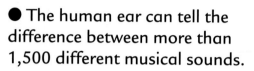

Amazing facts

● The human ear can tell the difference between more than 1,500 different musical sounds.

☆ *Every night, you grow a little longer as the discs between the bones in your back stretch. During the day, you shrink back to your usual height.*

● Did you know that you blink about 20,000 times a day? Blinking helps to wash dust and germs from your eyes.

☆ *Your body sheds tiny flakes of skin all the time. Every year, you shed about 200 grams of dead skin. Most house dust is really made up of dead skin.*

● Your hair grows faster in the morning than it does at night.

☆ *Did you know that your bones are not made of the strongest material in your body? The tough outer covering on your teeth, called enamel, is stronger.*

● The smallest bone in your body is in your ear. It is called the stirrup and is only about the size of a pea!

☆ *Inside your head, you have around 14,000 million brain cells. These control everything that your body does.*

● A sip of milk takes just six seconds to travel from your mouth to your stomach. Food takes up to 24 hours to pass through your body.

☆ *When you sneeze, you force air out of your lungs at a speed of up to 165km per hour. This is faster than a hurricane!*

● Did you know that you have the same number of bones in your neck as a giraffe? Seven!

☆ *The human body can stay alive for three weeks without food, but only a few minutes without oxygen.*

Glossary

blood A thick liquid which flows around your body. Blood is made up of watery fluid, red blood cells and **white blood cells.**

blood vessels Tubes that carry **blood** around the body.

bones The hard white parts inside your body that make up your skeleton.

brain The control centre of your body.

carbon dioxide A **waste** gas your body makes when it uses **oxygen**. Your **blood** carries it to your **lungs** and you breathe it out.

cell A tiny living unit. All living things are made up of cells.

energy The strength to do things.

germ A tiny living thing that can make you sick.

heart The **muscle** that pumps **blood** around your body.

lungs You breathe in and out with your lungs.

muscles Parts inside your body which help move your **bones** and make your food tubes work.

nerves Parts that carry messages to and from your **brain**.

oxygen A gas in the air. Oxygen goes into your **lungs** when you breathe in. Then it passes from your lungs into your **blood** and travels to all parts of your body.

senses The powers which make you aware of the world around you. Your five senses are sight, hearing, touch, smell and taste.

temperature How hot or cold something is.

vitamins and minerals Substances found in food. You need them to keep you healthy.

waste Something your body doesn't need.

white blood cells Parts of your **blood** that destroy **germs**.

Index

Published by Two-Can Publishing,
43-45 Dorset Street, London W1U 7NA

© 2001 Two-Can Publishing

For information on Two-Can books and multimedia, call (0)20 7224 2440, fax (0)20 7224 7005, or visit our website at http://www.two-canpublishing.com

Text: Rachel Wright
Consultant: Dr R Ibrahim
Watercolour artwork: Stuart Trotter
Computer artwork: D Oliver
Commissioned photography: Steve Gorton
Photo research: Dipika Palmer-Jenkins
Editorial Director: Lorraine Estelle
Project Manager: Eljay Yildirim
Editor: Deborah Kespert
Assistant Editors: Julia Hillyard and Claire Yude
Co-edition Editor: Leila Peerun

'Two-Can' is a trademark of Two-Can Publishing. Two-Can Publishing is a division of Zenith Entertainment Ltd, 43-45 Dorset Street, London W1U 7NA

Hardback ISBN 1-85434-
Paperback ISBN 1-85434-967-8

Dewey Decimal Classification 612

Hardback 2 4 6 8 10 9 7 5 3 1
Paperback 2 4 6 8 10 9 7 5 3 1

A catalogue record for this book is available from the British Library.

Printed in Spain by Graficromo S.A.

Photographic credits: Britstock-IFA (Weststock, David Perry) p11tr, (Bernd Ducke) p18-19c; Steve Gorton p7, p15,

Title previously published under the Launch Pad Library series

CAS

msc

ROTHERHAM PUBLIC LIBRARIES

GROWING UP

by Karen Bryant-Mole

Consultant: John Hall,
Counselling Support Manager of ChildLine

Wayland

Adoption
Bullying
Child Abuse
Death
Growing Up
Splitting Up
Step Families

Designed by Helen White
Edited by Deb Elliott

We gratefully acknowledge the assistance of Dr Rachel Waugh, Principal Clinical
Psychologist, Great Ormond Street Hospital

First published in 1993 by Wayland (Publishers) Limited
61 Western Road, Hove, East Sussex BN3 1JD

British Library Cataloguing in Publication Data
Bryant-Mole, Karen
  Growing Up. – (What's Happening? Series)
  I. Title II. Series
  612.6

ISBN 0 7502 0878 3

Phototypeset by White Design
Printed by G. Canale & C. S. p. A, Turin
Bound in France by A. G. M.

CONTENTS

All of the people who are featured in this book are models. We gratefully acknowledge the help and assistance of all those individuals who have been involved in this project.

WHAT'S IT ALL ABOUT?

ABOVE *Puberty is something that all children go through. It is part of growing up.*

Human beings need to be able to make more human beings. If we couldn't then, after a while, there would be no more people. This 'making more' is called reproduction.

Many of the changes that your body goes through in the time between being a child and being an adult are to do with getting your body ready, so that you can play your part in the making of another human being. This doesn't mean that you have to have babies, it just means that you can.

That time between being a child and being an adult is sometimes called puberty or adolescence. Children start puberty at different times. A few begin puberty as young as eight or nine years old. Other children may not start until they are fifteen or sixteen. Some children who start puberty early worry about it, perhaps because they think it makes them different to their friends. In the same way, some fifteen year olds who haven't yet begun puberty worry because they think that there must be something wrong with them. There is nothing wrong or different about starting either early or late. Your body will begin to change when it is ready.

There is more to growing up than having a changing body. Growing up also involves starting to make up your own mind about things and making your own choices. You will probably start to experience much stronger feelings about yourself and other people.

BELOW
Different children start puberty at different times.

HOW IT STARTS

Richard and his family were going to a wedding. Richard decided to wear the trousers that he had worn to a party a couple of months before. But when he put them on they were far too short. Either the trousers had shrunk or he had grown!

It was Richard who had grown. A short spell of fast growth is often one of the first signs of puberty. Growing is something that can be seen, but puberty is actually started by something that can't be seen at all – hormones. Hormones are chemicals which are made in one part of your body but which travel to other parts of your body and make them develop. It is hormones made in your brain that start the process of puberty.

Growing fast is not always the first sign of puberty. You might find that the first sign is the appearance of hair between your legs and under your arms. Or, if you are a girl, it may be that your breasts start to develop. A girl's hips usually get wider during puberty, too. The body changes in a boy mean that your voice will deepen and your penis and testicles will get bigger.

6

The thing to remember about all this growing and changing is that boys and girls, men and women, come in all shapes and sizes. There is no 'right' way to look. Your body is as individual as you are.

BELOW We all look different and have different body shapes.

AM I NORMAL?

Yasmin was interested in how her body was changing, so she borrowed a book from the library about it. The book was full of useful information and drawings.

In both boys and girls, the parts of your body that are between your legs are called genitals. If you are a girl you will probably have realized that it's rather difficult to look at your own genitals, unless you are an acrobat! So Yasmin, very sensibly, sat herself down with a mirror, to see if she could work out where all the bits that the book mentioned were. She looked in the mirror but what she saw didn't look anything like the picture in the book. Yasmin was really upset. She thought there must be something wrong with her.

BELOW Yasmin found a book that told her about the human body.

The drawings of bodies in books are often simple line drawings, called diagrams. Usually they are used to name different parts of your body and to show you where those parts are. They are not meant to look exactly like the real thing. Your own genitals may not look as neat and tidy as those in a diagram.

If you are a boy you might be worrying about your genitals too. Many boys are concerned about the length of their penis. But it doesn't actually matter how long it is. A long penis is no better or worse than a shorter one. If your penis hasn't grown at all, then all this means is that your body isn't yet ready to begin puberty.

We all have two eyes, a nose and a mouth. Yet eyes, noses and mouths can come in very different shapes and sizes. In the same way, we all have the various parts that make up our genitals, but they too come in different shapes and sizes.

ABOVE We all worry about how we look from time to time. Sometimes we compare ourselves to others and feel that we don't 'match up'. We all have different qualities. That's what makes us special.

9

BODY HAIR

Chris and his parents had talked about how his body would change as he grew older. He knew that one of the first things he might notice would be hair starting to grow around his genitals.

In both boys and girls, the hair that grows around your genitals is called pubic hair. Chris was a bit surprised because, although the hair on his head was straight and light brown, the first few pubic hairs that grew seemed to be much darker and slightly curly. At first it didn't bother him, but then as more hairs grew they seemed to be getting curlier, darker and more wiry. This worried Chris, so he asked his dad about it. His dad was able to reassure him that pubic hair often looks and feels different to the hair on your head.

You will also find that hair will start to grow under your arms during puberty. Usually underarm hair only starts to grow after you've started growing pubic hair, but for a few children underarm hair might be the first sign of puberty. Most children find that the hairs on their arms and legs get darker too.

During puberty boys begin to grow hair on their faces. This usually happens after their genitals have developed fully. So don't worry if your body has started to change but there is still no sign of any facial hair, it will start to grow in time.

BELOW At first, the hair that grows on your face will probably be quite soft.

PERIODS

OPPOSITE *Some girls feel a bit down, or have stomachache during their periods. It's quite normal, so don't worry if you react in either, or both, of these ways.*

Emma's mum felt that it was time to talk to Emma about one of the most important changes that happens to a girl's body – starting periods. She explained that Emma had lots of tiny egg cells stored inside her body and that, during puberty, her body would start to release these cells. Every month one cell would travel into her uterus. The lining of the uterus would thicken with blood. The lining would then break up and come out through her vagina. She told Emma that it usually takes about five days for the blood to trickle out, but that it can take more time or less.

Emma wanted to know how much blood there would be. Her mum said that it was only a couple of tablespoons altogether, but that it might feel like more. She explained to Emma that the blood can be soaked up either in a pad or in a tampon which fits inside your vagina. Emma decided she'd rather try with pads first. Emma was worried about starting her periods when she was at school, and she was frightened in case the blood came through on to her clothes and everyone saw it. Her mum suggested that Emma kept a pad in her schoolbag. She also said that she thought Emma would feel the dampness, and be able to get to the loo, well before any blood came through on to her clothes.

Most girls start their periods about one or two years after their breasts have started to develop, but some start earlier or later than this. You may begin to notice a white discharge from your vagina. This is a good sign that your body is starting to make the changes that lead up to your first period.

WET DREAMS

Luke shared a bedroom with his older brother, Scott. One morning Luke noticed Scott taking the duvet cover off his bed. 'What are you doing?' asked Luke, 'Have you wet the bed?' 'No, I haven't.' Scott said. 'If you must know, I had a wet dream.' Luke was really interested. He'd never heard of wet dreams. He asked his brother to tell him what they were.

Scott explained that, during puberty, boys start to get erections. He told Luke that an erection is when your penis gets pumped full of blood. This makes it grow bigger and become hard. It points upwards instead of hanging downwards. He also said that during puberty, boys' bodies start to make a white, sticky liquid called semen. When a penis is erect, semen can squirt out of the penis. This is called ejaculation. Scott explained that a wet dream means you get an erection and ejaculate while you are asleep.

Luke wanted to know whether you only get erections in your sleep. His brother told him that you could get them at other times too. Sometimes you can make yourself have an erection by stroking or touching your penis and sometimes erections happen all by themselves. An erection that happens by itself is called a spontaneous erection. Luke wondered whether having a spontaneous erection was embarrassing. Scott said that at first he was embarrassed because he thought other people might notice, but that he'd got more used to them now and he knew that most of his friends had them too.

BELOW Most boys have spontaneous erections at some time. Don't worry if you do. It's quite normal and other people usually don't notice.

YOUR SKIN

Kirsty was babysitting for Rebecca. The girls were watching television together. As Kirsty got up to get Rebecca a drink, she caught sight of herself in a mirror. 'Oh no,' she groaned, 'I can see them from here!'. Rebecca wanted to know what she was talking about. 'Spots!' said Kirsty. I can't get rid of them. No one will like me!' Rebecca told Kirsty that it didn't matter to her whether Kirsty had spots or not. She said that she liked Kirsty because she was kind and fun to be with. Rebecca thought it would be silly not to like someone just because of a few spots!

Many people find that their skin becomes more oily during puberty. This oiliness can clog up your skin and cause spots. Some skins seem to make spots more easily than others and you may not be able to do anything to stop the spots coming. But, as spots are often the result of too much oil, you may find it helps if you keep the skin as oil-free as possible by washing well, especially around your face and back. Spots usually go away in time, but, if they are very bad, you might find it helpful to talk to your doctor about them.

You will probably also find that your skin begins to make sweat, especially under your arms and around your genitals. It is important to keep these areas clean as old sweat does not smell very pleasant. If you choose to, you might like to use an antiperspirant or a deodorant under your arms.

BELOW Try not to worry about having spots. There is much more to you than your skin.

OPPOSITE Keeping your skin as oil-free as possible by washing it every evening and morning may help to stop spots coming.

PARENTS

Sam wanted to go into town on the bus, but his mum and dad said he couldn't go because he was too young to be out on his own. They all got very cross about it and it ended up with his dad shouting and Sam stamping off to his bedroom.

Sam thought his parents were just trying to spoil his fun, but they weren't really being mean on purpose. They were worried about Sam. He had never been to town by himself, so, the way they saw it, they had said no because they loved Sam and were protecting him. Sam's parents calmed down. After a lot of thought they decided to let him go as long as he promised to be back on the 4:15 bus.

If Sam came back on time, how do you think his parents would feel about letting him go out on his own another time? How would they feel if he missed the bus because he couldn't be bothered to keep an eye on the time?

As you grow up you may find that you have more arguments with your parents. If it is an argument about something you want or don't want to do, try to talk about it. Explain why it is important to you and listen to what your parents have to say about it too. A shouting match is unlikely to solve anything. A proper discussion and a bit of give and take may keep everyone happy.

RIGHT Don't be too hard on your mum and dad. It can be difficult for parents to get used to the fact that their child is growing up.

18

FRIENDS

Everyone likes to be liked and feel part of a group, but sometimes it's important to ask yourself why you are friends with a particular group of people. Good reasons include liking each other, having fun together and trusting each other. Less good reasons for being friends include only being friends because you are scared of them, and being frightened of what they would do or say if you weren't their friend.

BELOW Heather started smoking because her best friend smoked.

Heather had just started smoking. She didn't like the taste or the smell of cigarettes, but she smoked because her best friend smoked and she didn't want to be different. It can be very difficult, but learning how to say no to things that you don't really want to do is an important part of growing up. You might find it helpful to read up about things like smoking and drugs so that, if you are asked to do something you'd rather not do, you can say why you don't want to do it.

Lots of people find it very important to be the same as their friends. They like to wear the same sort of clothes, listen to the same music and act in the same way. And that's alright. But you are an individual too. You don't always have to agree with everyone else or do the same things as everyone else. And if someone says that they won't be your friend any more because you want to be different, then that person is not much of a friend.

ABOVE As you grow up you will probably find that your friends and other people your own age start to play a more important part in your life.

MOODS AND FEELINGS

Henry had an older sister called Clare, who was fourteen years old. They used to get on very well, but lately it seemed to Henry that everything he did or said was wrong. Henry felt very mixed up. How was it that Clare used to enjoy being with him but now nothing he did was right? He talked to his mum about it. She explained to Henry that Clare was growing up and that growing up can sometimes make you feel moody and fed up.

You may find that your moods and feelings change from day to day during puberty. Some days you might feel very happy. Other days you might feel like crying. Some days you might feel like being with your friends. Other days you might just want to be alone. Sometimes children who are not used to having such strong feelings find them a bit frightening. If you ever feel like this, do try to talk to someone about it. Coping with lots of new moods and feelings isn't just confusing for you, it can also be confusing for those around you. Most families try to be as under-standing as possible, but they cannot guess how you are feeling. Talking about your feelings may help both them and you.

It is your hormones that are behind all these mood changes. Hormones don't just make your body grow and develop, they affect your emotions too. When your hormones settle down, your feelings will probably settle down too.

OPPOSITE Henry's sister sometimes got cross and fed up with him.

BELOW Sometimes you may feel like being on your own.

23

CRUSHES

BELOW *You may find yourself having strong feelings about someone. That person may not feel the same way about you.*

OPPOSITE *Christine loves reading about André Agassi and looking at pictures of him.*

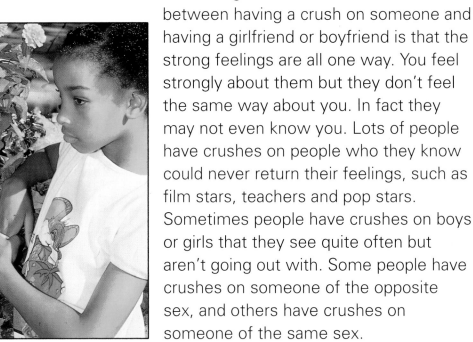

Christine's bedroom is covered in posters of her favourite sports star. Every time she sees him on television she gets a funny, excited feeling in her stomach. Her most treasured possession is a signed photograph of him. Christine daydreams about him and she tells all her friends that she is in love with him.

Having strong feelings like this about someone is sometimes called having a crush. The difference between having a crush on someone and having a girlfriend or boyfriend is that the strong feelings are all one way. You feel strongly about them but they don't feel the same way about you. In fact they may not even know you. Lots of people have crushes on people who they know could never return their feelings, such as film stars, teachers and pop stars. Sometimes people have crushes on boys or girls that they see quite often but aren't going out with. Some people have crushes on someone of the opposite sex, and others have crushes on someone of the same sex.

Crushes are a safe way of finding out about the strong feelings that you start to experience during puberty. Crushes can be a lot of fun, but it is important to remember that the person you have your crush on is unlikely to feel the same way about you. Enjoy the feelings that having a crush on someone can bring, but don't lose touch with reality.

25

BOYFRIENDS AND GIRLFRIENDS

ABOVE *Simon and his girlfriend, Amy, are both sixteen years old.*

Jake's big brother Simon had started going out with a girl called Amy. Jake knew that boys often have girlfriends and girls often have boyfriends, but there was something bothering him. Jake was nine. He had lots of friends but all his friends were boys. Jake couldn't imagine ever wanting to go out with a girl.

When children are very young they usually play in mixed groups of girls and boys. When they get to school, many children start forming groups of friends that tend to be made up mostly of either girls or boys. Quite a lot of children end up only having friends the same sex as themselves. But puberty often changes all this. As well as affecting your moods, your hormones are likely to make you start having strong feelings about girls or boys.

On top of this, some of the body changes that happen to you are designed to make you more attractive to the opposite sex. So, instead of only having friends the same sex as themselves, most girls and boys start to have friends of the opposite sex too.

Sometimes people worry about how they can get someone to like them. They think they have to act in a certain way or agree with everything the other person says. But the best way to get on with someone is to be yourself and do and say the things you feel are right.

LEFT You can have a friend who is a girl or a friend who is a boy without them being your girlfriend or boyfriend.

TALKING ABOUT GROWING UP

ABOVE You might find it helpful to talk to your friends about how you are feeling.

If you have questions about growing up, do try to talk to someone, your mum or dad perhaps. They might find this a bit difficult at first. This is not because there is anything wrong with growing up, but because it's not something that people are very good at talking about. Sometimes they might want to work out the best way of answering your questions, so they may not be able to give you answers straight away. If your parents refuse to answer your questions, you could try asking a teacher or some other adult who you trust. It is important to get your information from people who know what they are talking about. Children hear a lot of things about growing up from other children. Some of it may be true, but a lot of it is made up or exaggerated. If someone tells you something that worries you or something that doesn't seem to make any sense, try to ask an adult about it. If you have a good friend you may find that it helps to share your

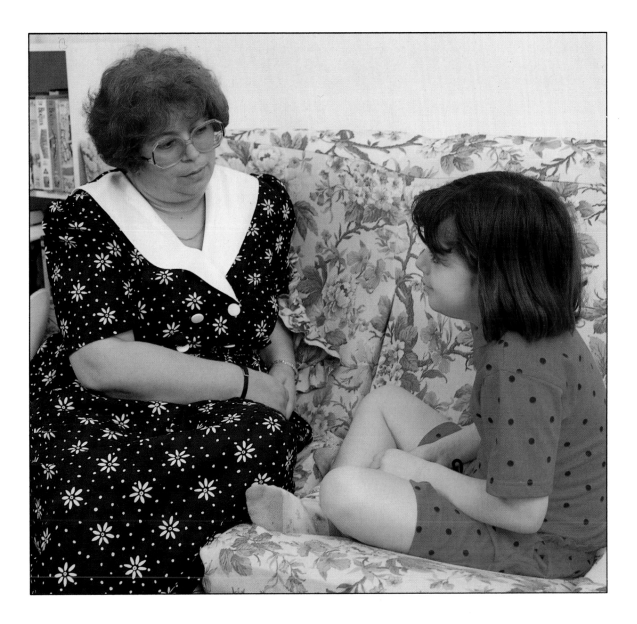

feelings with him or her. And there may be some things that you feel able to talk to your friend about that you couldn't talk about with anyone else.

Growing up can be a confusing time, but it can also be an exciting time. It's a bit like a wobbly rope bridge that links being a child and being an adult. Some parts are fun, other parts might be a bit worrying, but everyone gets to the other side in the end!

ABOVE If you have any questions about growing up, ask someone.

FOR PARENTS AND TEACHERS

As they grow up, many children become acutely aware of their changing bodies. Negative comments about their bodies, even when said light-heartedly, can be extremely hurtful. Children are bombarded by media images of the 'perfect' body. You, as parents and teachers, can help by reassuring children that people come in all shapes and sizes and that your particular shape and size is part of what makes you, you. Another way of helping children to feel happy with their bodies is to make sure they know that they are valued as people. Children who feel good about themselves are less likely to worry about their bodies than those who feel inadequate.

Try to be open and honest with your child. There will be many things that your child would like to talk about and questions that he or she needs to have answered. If you refuse to answer these questions your child may feel angry with you for letting him or her down. If you react by being embarrassed or disgusted your child may feel guilty or ashamed.

Adolescence can be a difficult time for parents as well as for children. Your child will probably want to become more and more independent, while you will probably be concerned about his or her safety and well-being. Keeping all lines of communication open and expressing your feelings as well as listening to the views of your child may be more productive than a dogged refusal to allow your child to do something.

One of the most important things that parents or teachers can do to help children through puberty is to make sure they know that you are there for them. They need to know that you won't reject them, that they can talk to you about anything and that you like and respect them.

GLOSSARY

Breasts The two glands on a woman's chest. The glands produce milk when the woman has a baby, which the baby feeds on.

Exaggerated To have made something seem greater or more important than it really is.

Genitals The parts of men's and women's bodies which are between their legs.

Individual To be your own person, with your own ideas, thoughts and way of dressing, for example.

Penis Part of a boy's genitals.

Semen A fluid which comes out of a man's penis. Semen contains sperm which are needed to make babies.

Testicles The two glands which hang down on either side of a boy's penis. Sperm are made and stored in the testicles.

Uterus Another name for the womb. It is the part of a woman's body where a baby grows and develops for nine months, until it is ready to be born.

Vagina An opening between a girl's legs, which leads to the womb where a baby grows until it is ready to be born.

BOOKS TO READ

Talking About AIDS by Karen Bryant-Mole (Wayland, 1993)
The Human Cycle by Nina Morgan (Wayland, 1993)

INDEX

Picture Acknowledgements

Sally and Richard Greenhill 10, 11, 17, 20, 25, 27; Images Colour Library 4, 26; Zul Mukhida / Chapel Studios cover, 6, 14, 16, 18-19, 22; Rex Features 14-15; Paul Seheult 8; Skjold 4-5, 7, 9, 13, 20, 21, 23, 24, 28, 29.